THE BAHAMAS

FLORIDA

Little Bahama Bank LITTLE ABACO

GRAND BAHAMA

GREAT ABACO

Northwest Providence Channel

BIMINI
ISLANDS

ELEUTHERA

Nassau

NEW PROVIDENCE

Great Bahama Bank

Cay Sal Bank

ANDROS

Tongue of the Ocean

Exuma Sound

CAT ISLAND

CONCEPTION
ISLAND

SAN SALVADOR

EXUMA

RUM CAY

SAMANA CAY

LONG
ISLAND

CROOKED ISLAND

RAGGED
ISLAND

MAYAGUANA

CUBA

*Hogsty
Reef*

ACKLINS

Abraham's
Bay

Caicos Passage

GRAND TURK

TURKS &
CAICOS

GREAT INAGUA

Mouchoir Bank

Silver Bank

HAITI

DOMINICAN REPUBLIC

Children
of the
Sea

Exploring the marine diversity of The Bahamas and the Caribbean

Nicolas and Dragan Popov

First published 2000 by
MACMILLAN EDUCATION LTD
London and Oxford
Companies and representatives throughout the world

ISBN 0-333-73538-2

10 9 8 7 6 5 4 3 2 1
09 08 07 06 05 04 03 02 01 00

This book is printed on paper suitable for recycling and
made from fully managed and sustained forest sources.

Colour separation by Tenon & Polort Colour Scanning Ltd

Printed in Hong Kong

A catalogue record of this book is available from the
British Library.

Photographs by Nicolas and Dragan Popov except page 53 bottom
(Philip Dutton, Island Expedition) and page 72 (Sam Faccioli,
Island Expedition)

Designed by Alex Tucker Holbrook Design (Oxford) Limited

Contents

Acknowledgements

Dedication – *To Mama Brigitte*

We would like to take this opportunity to make a special dedication to all Island Expedition team members and students who took part in our expeditions at sea and made them so challenging and rewarding.

WE WISH TO THANK our publishers, Macmillan Education Ltd, Sir Nicholas Nuttall, Bt. of BREEF for the Foreword, Christopher Hill of Island Expedition 98 for the drawings and Jane Popov for her helpful editing and proofreading.

In the last 15 years a number of individuals, companies, institutions and organizations have contributed to Island Expedition in the form of funds, scholarships, equipment and support on land and/or sea. There would never be enough space on this page to acknowledge all those who, one way or another, have been involved with the project. Only major contributors and/or those who have shown continued support are listed:

American Airlines, Ad Works, Caroline Antic, AOM, Apex, Archives (Bahamas), ASA Pritchard, Bahamas Copier, Bahamas Ministry of (Tourism, Education and Foreign Affairs), Bahamasair, Frank and Gisa Banks, Richard and Susan Barnes, BASRA, Bay Street Garage, Richard Beek, Benetton, Tchoupette Bernstein, BREEF, Paula Brennen, Brown's Boat Basin, Kelly Bryan, Rob and Robin Burr, Clean Islands International, Club Med, College of the Bahamas, Courtney Curtis, Credit Suisse (Bahamas), Dayne and Linda D'Aguilar, D'Albenas Agency, Laetitia Dablanc, Darier Hentsch Trust, Ray and Evelyn Darville, Len and Celia Davies, Renato and Anna De Paolis, Amandine Defrasne, Richard Dolamore, John Deleveaux, Department of Fisheries, Medi Dubaut, Hon. Ivy Dumont, Sam and Tony Duncomb, Philip Dutton, East Bay Marina, Sandra Eneas, Reno Eneas, Family Guardian Insurance, Mike Ferrara, Ferrier Lullin Trust, Alain and Sophie Gayot, Mistral Girardeau, Marshall Golnick, Agnes Guyon, Peggy Hall, Marie Hastrais, Divers Haven, Tony Hepburn, Linda Hubert, Island Merchants, Thomas Kessler, Emerick and Patou Knowles, Ricardo Knowles, Jagar, Henri Jean, Mary Jenkins, Dr Portia Jordan, Lions Club (Nassau), Lyford Cay Foundation, Brendon Lynch, Pericles Maillis, Minouche Marvel, Claude Mascioni, George and Yvonne Menoud, Miami Boatshow, Brendan Moorchcad, Monaco Oceanographic Museum, Bill Moore, Morley Realty, *Nassau Guardian*, Nassau Restaurant Supplies, Nassau SCUBA Center, Nautica Inflatables, Kevin O'Sullivan and family, Benedict Petit, Elisa Orduy, Keith and Sara Parker, Private Trust, Puerto Rico Tourism, Purity Bakery, Danah Quimby, Anne Rebardy, Rock n' Roll Café, Stephanie Rosse, Rotary Club of East Nassau, Marie-Christine Roux, Sailorman, Dr Gail Saunders, Neil Sealey, Timo Serraz, Shell Bahamas Ltd, SOS Grand Bleu, *Southern Boating Magazine*, Stanford University, Stuart Cove Diving, Gary Sweeting, *Tribune*, Tsavoussis brothers, Ira Tytle, UK Sailing Academy, UNESCO, UNEP, University of Miami, John Vandershoot and family, Bertrand Wache, Rhonda Walker, Warren Watson, Kathy Weech, *What's On*, Gail Woon, Yamaha Outboards, Zonta Club (Monaco).

One can never forget the support of our family and friends: Brigitte Popov who helped with many expedition departures and had to put up with the coming and going of hundreds of students; Marco Popov and family and Elizabeth Sydenham for their ongoing support; our dearest friends Dick and Buffy Hart, our Miami connection; Patricia De Latorre, our California connection; Joan Mann, our Exumas connection; and Paul L. Knowles, our Bahama connection. Finally to the memories of our friends Gina Oliver, Ossie Brown and Tony McKay (Exuma), and to all of you, thank you.

THE SEA is a wonderful teacher and the Popovs are the best of guides to her classroom. They have learned a great deal themselves from the sea and their lives are devoted to passing on that knowledge. They do so not for selfish reasons, but to recruit others so that together we may, by restoring the sea, secure our future. To make their work even more attractive they have chosen to work in one of the most beautiful parts of the ocean, a place where people are already beginning the restoration work.

Most of us learn best when all our senses are engaged. We are predators and we learn, like any other predator, when we are alert and on our toes. We pay particular attention when we are at risk, as land animals always are offshore. We know that if we make a simple mistake in ship handling, navigation or if we run out of fuel or water at sea the consequences can at worst be fatal. After a few days at sea with excellent seamen like the Popovs, we begin to learn quickly, permanently and happily. But for all their skills, the Popovs are only guides, they can open the book of the sea for you and tell you where to look – what you learn from it is your affair.

Learning from the sea is utterly different from learning from a book. The authors, the animals who keep the book of marine life up to date, do not mind if they 'sell' you a copy or not, nor are they trying to pass on some message like a human author. You will never finish the book, know how it began or how it will end, but unlike any book by a human author, everything in it is true. The natural world is a place of constant examination, pass or fail – eat or be eaten. The survivors are living proof that they have the right answers. The wily barracuda, steadfast mangrove and patient polyp do not give up their secrets easily but they are there if you have the skill and patience to tease them out. You will often be deceived by speed or stillness, dazzled by colour or confused by camouflage; but if you work at it you will find something you need. It is both the oldest book of life, reflecting with pinpoint accuracy what worked in the past, and as up to the minute as the latest stock market quotation.

At present, as you will see from the introduction to *Children of the Sea*, it tells a sad story. Man is taking too many living things out of the sea and putting too much poison into it. We need to remember that in the past when there were great extinctions, like the end of the dinosaurs, it was the top predators, those who depend on the so-called lower organisms for their food, who perished. You could say that we are destroying a great part of the Book of Life and history shows that those who destroy knowledge, the book burners, deserve their gruesome fate.

Do not despair. There is still time. The pressure of our increasing numbers, our tendency to migrate towards the sea (most people live within 100 miles of the sea's edge), and our appetite for food, fresh water and raw materials, will peak in about 35 years' time. Learn from the sea, convince as many others as you can that what you have learned is true and we will come through the crunch. Already we know what must be done; it is a question of will and of courage. Like the coral polyps, which have so far built the largest structures ever made by living things, we can learn to build, restore and work together to a beautiful natural pattern. Learn how they do it, what conditions are essential to their survival, and you will know how to proceed.

It will not be easy however. It is very hard for us to know what is going on in the sea. Compared to a sea-going mammal like a dolphin or a whale, let alone a fish, underwater we are blind, blinkered, sluggish, speechless, short of breath and almost deaf. Even on the surface we are at the mercy of wind, wave and tide, weaker than the youngest gull or penguin. But we are, thanks to the amazing brains we have inherited, capable of observing, learning and choosing what we do next. The coral polyp cannot choose. It goes on for countless generations building billions of identical calcium carbonate skeletons in a set pattern and it will go on doing so until the conditions in the sea change and become impossible for corals to live there any more. This has happened in the past after great natural changes, which we call disasters, and will certainly happen again before the world ends. What a tragedy it would be if the beautiful reefs and all the species that depend on them died, not from natural causes, but at our careless hands.

For billions of years life in the sea has adapted to changing conditions. We see the survivors. Through guides and teachers like the Popovs, we can learn from them. We must, for our survival as a species depends on it.

SIR NICHOLAS NUTTALL, BT.

Decline of the Oceans

THE OCEANS OF THE WORLD are the heart of the living body – Planet Earth. On a global level oceans regulate temperature, produce oxygen, absorb carbon dioxide, control the weather and provide the atmosphere with most of the moisture that drops back on the land. Ninety-seven per cent of all the water on earth is from the seas and oceans and water covers nearly three-quarters of the earth's surface. The ocean is earth's life-support system, without it there would be no life on earth.

However, as we begin this new millennium, there is still so much unknown and undiscovered about the oceans. It seems that many of the new technologies developed in the last fifty years have been concentrated in the heavens. For example, by studying supernovas trillions of miles away we may be able to determine if our universe is shrinking or growing. But how important is it to determine the fate of the earth in a million years' time when the next hundred years seem so uncertain?

What we do know today is that this huge volume of sea water is poisoned by the waste products of man. If you trace the toxins found in the ocean, the overwhelming majority lead back to land. Proper management of our resources on land and in the seas is therefore of utmost importance if we wish to maintain a healthy and sustainable existence on our watery planet.

For hundreds of millions of years animals and plants have had to adapt to changes in their environment and to competition with each other. The fittest survived and evolved with the changes, while others became extinct and only remain in the fossil records. Some marine animals, like corals, were seriously affected by major geological and climatic changes, but they have survived the forces of nature and periods of mass extinctions for 500 million years.

Today the environment of The Bahamas and the Caribbean is threatened more by man than by any natural event it may have faced in the past. In contrast to slower natural changes it is important to understand that animals and plants cannot tolerate faster man-made changes.

The people of the Bahamas and Caribbean islands are very dependent on the sea for their tourism and fishing industries. Visitors from around the world choose these islands because of their inherent beauty. But unfortunately this beauty is changing. Human population and unsustainable development are impacting the environment, together threatening each island's wildlife, habitats and its value to people as a continued source of revenue. Some of the visible and long-lasting harm to islands comes in the form of dumping garbage and waste into the sea, overly efficient fishing practices, harvesting and hunting of endangered marine animals, careless diving methods and altering the naturally rich habitats.

Education and the study of our marine ecosystems is the key to conservation of the sea. *Children of the Sea* is an effort in environmental education. The goal of the book is to teach students, islanders and visitors about basic ecological concepts and threats to the marine environment of the Caribbean Sea. The section on marine ecosystems covers the three principal areas: coral reefs, mangroves and sand and sea grass terrains. Included in each ecosystem is a description of its species diversity, function, structural aspects and degradation due to human impact. Specific sections on the humpback whales of the Silver Bank and dolphins of The Bahamas are the result of extensive observations and studies completed over a 10 year period.

Throughout this book you will find quotes, stories and poems written by students on the Island Expedition School at Sea programme, which offers the possibility for students to learn directly in the field in various environments (ocean, banks, reef, mangroves, coastal and inland). Along with its educational programme, the non-profit organization carries out research on marine mammals, surveys of coral reef and mangrove ecosystems, analysis of marine debris and general ethnographic studies of each island visited.

It is time that we all become aware of our impact on the environment. We need to understand how the web of life connects the small unicellular algae to the great humpback whale. We need to understand the fragility of nature and its importance, not just to tourism and fishing industries, but to our very existence. When you protect the environment you protect yourself.

The continued disrespect for the ocean could translate into the collapse of key industries such as tourism and fishing.

How can we guarantee a clean and bountiful sea for these children fishing on the dock of Staniel Cay in The Bahamas? By heightening our own awareness, and teaching our children about the intricate balance of life in the ocean, we can strive to protect it. Let us remember that life is said to have begun in the sea; we are all children of the sea.

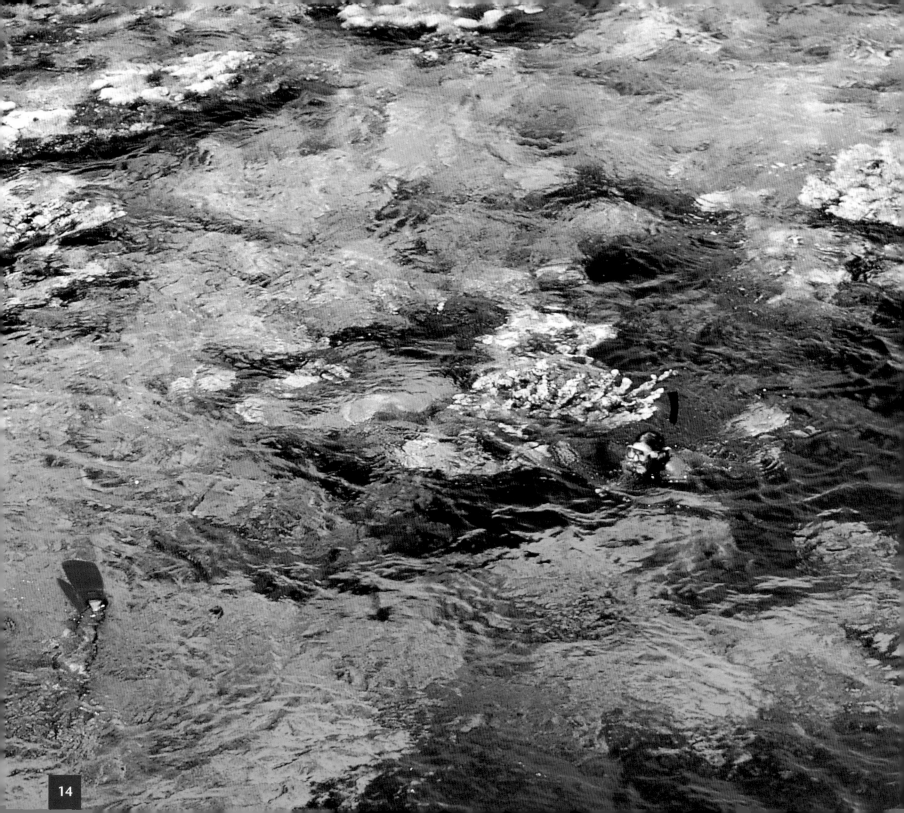

Island Expedition

IN JUNE 1985, recent college graduates Dragan and Nicolas Popov established Island Expedition. With two donated Nautica inflatables and several small university grants the team set off from its base in Nassau to explore the communities of the northern Bahamas. Armed with fishing gear, basic provisions, tents, photographic and recording equipment, the team began documenting the fascinating lives of Bahamian people in areas still largely untouched by the modern world. The team then was small, made up of university students who shared a sense of adventure and a desire to document a life style on the brink of permanent change.

Travelling in tiny boats no bigger than yacht tenders necessitated camping on beaches or in communities. Often the 4.5 metre inflatables would be met by perplexed locals with the question 'Where's 'de big boat, mon?' The shallow draft allowed exploration of places seldom seen by outsiders and after several months, hundreds of hours of taped interviews and thousands of documentary photos the first book was published was financed largely by sponsors and advertising space.

Thousands of miles later, the expedition has grown and changed. The use of sailboats facilitates larger numbers of participants, but rigid bottom inflatables are still used to explore inaccessible regions and the teams camp on the shore whenever possible. The new emphasis for the expedition is on teaching school-aged children under the guidance of college graduates.

The expedition experience reaches far beyond the relatively small numbers of youths who have been directly involved on the sea. Regular presentations in schools and colleges, production of books, articles and films and participation in world-level conferences and expositions have all been aimed at increasing environmental awareness.

Pushing off to sea on one of the original expeditions

Use of small inflatables allowed the team to access isolated shallow banks. These tents were definitely set up at high tide

School at Sea

THE SCHOOL at Sea, open to children aged 12 to 17 and college students, is perhaps the most exciting and enriching part of the Island Expedition experience. Children of different colour, social background and culture are enrolled from many parts of the world. Financial hardship does not prevent participation as sponsors can be found for underprivileged children. Furthermore, each expedition includes a few troubled youths. Nature is the strongest healer, especially for youths in need of direction. The experience they have on the sea often gives them a new perspective which stays with them and aids reintegration.

Students learn 'hands-on' through exposure to a wide range of information and situations. The School at Sea programme is a 24 hours a day, 7 days a week experience. The strength of the School at Sea lies in its informal structure which gives the children the opportunity to learn, grow and develop at every level. The often harsh environment of the ocean and the basic way of life experienced on expedition demands a lot of the young participants.

School work on board the Simpatico

STUDENTS ARE GIVEN THE OPPORTUNITY to live aboard a sailing vessel for as long as 6 months, navigating through some of the most challenging regions and exploring islands along the way. Every participant gets plenty of opportunity to learn the rudiments of sailing and boat handling on a daily basis, with running repairs and engine maintainance a regular part of the experience. Often students spend many days hard at work in the boatyard preparing for the long journey ahead. At the beginning of an expedition this is an ideal way for the multicultural groups to start getting to know each other.

Once at sea there is the discipline of helming rotas and the extra safety measures needed during night crossings. For many it is a very daunting experience to be woken from their bunk in the middle of the night to take control of the helm.

The Caribbean seas are not always the smooth calm waters many imagine. The youngsters endure the challenge of storms and those lucky enough to be impervious to sea sickness learn to take care of the others.

An encounter with sperm whales during an ocean passage

Juan and José from Puerto Rico sheeting in the mainsail

Concentrating on keeping a steady course with team mates from four different nations standing by

Running repairs are a regular part of expedition activities

*With the sun setting, students prepare for a night sail aboard the **Simpatico***

Students get plenty of experience handling boat tenders

Sleeping off a heavy storm

Of all the watches, for me the most
pleasurable was the night watch and
navigation because it gives you a great
opportunity to think. It is incredible
to look up at all the stars and think
about all the planets and worlds that
we know nothing about. It makes you
think how little we are compared to the
rest of the universe and even this world.

FROM 'THE WATCH' BY LOUP VERGEZ, AGED 14, BELGIUM

Expedition students are expected to keep up with their regular school work

STUDENTS PARTICIPATE in a special one week orientation at the beginning of each expedition where local professors and visiting experts give lectures on subjects pertaining to the study programme. On expedition, a team of adults made up of graduates and professionals work with the students, ensuring they keep up with their regular school programme. One requirement of the School at Sea is that children organize to bring core school work with them so as not to fall behind when they return to their regular schools. Having the discipline to work from 8 a.m. until noon aboard the boat or on the beach requires daily supervision from one of the graduate tutors. Each tutor will take responsibility for a maximum of two students and is required to write reports for the schools.

As well as the daily demands of school work the students must submit a weekly assignment based on their experiences. This may take the form of a short essay, a poem or even a transcribed interview. Some choose to use the video camera to document a specific event. On the day the assignments are submitted, the whole team shares and comments on each other's work. This aspect has been particularly useful for youngsters with limited written skills – highly motivated by their rich experiences, they surprise themselves with the quality of their articles.

As the expedition travels, students are constantly exposed to numerous environments (pelagic-ocean, reef, mangrove, sand and sea grass and varied land coppice). Students are lectured on a wide range of topics, which are directly related to their practical experiences: survival skills; environmental issues and practice; data and research techniques; flora and fauna identification; and a knowledge of regional marine life. Often the lectures are given by experts working in the field who can share their research findings and generate a great deal of enthusiasm.

THE LOGISTICS of feeding and organizing as many as 25 people on the sea for several months can be quite challenging. The daily chores are given on a rota basis, a small team taking responsibility for all the chores on one particular day per week. The day starts with the rising sun. If the group are camping on the shore, firewood will have to be collected and vast pots of water set to boil. While travelling, tight galley space necessitates good organization and a great deal of patience. Apart from planning and preparing breakfast, lunch and dinner there is bread to be made and the expedition log book to update. Each team includes an adult, who will encourage the children to take on the decision making.

Before coming to the shipwreck which we now call home, we all had notions of how hard life would be. Simply living would be a challenge. Catching our own food, cooking over a fire, salt water baths, as well as sleeping in a hammock were all skills that we would need to master in order to survive. But once we got here it all seemed so easy. Comfort thrives here, at our new home, despite the fact we are living under such extreme circumstances. It seems crazy but it is true.

(FROM 'EXPEDITION=COMFORT' BY TAMARA BERKOWITZ, AGED 19, USA)

Amandine from France making an entry in the expedition log book

*Bahamian Wendell using the original oven of the **Polyxeni** wreck to bake bread and cakes. Improvisation is the key to survival when living aboard a wreck. (see section on whales)*

Adult volunteer Elisa (left) from Columbia helps students clean fish and conch

The day ends with a glowing fire and a full moon shining on the sea

Wᴵᵀᴴᴼᵁᵀ a regular supply of fresh fish the Expedition would have to suffer a constant round of tinned stew. Fortunately many of the students become keen fishermen and are proud of their expertise in providing for the group. During open water passages, lines are set and often just before sundown, when the failing light encourages fish from their hiding places, teams of students go out on fishing trips. In areas of sea grass, mature conchs are collected and cleaned – a lengthy and labour-intensive job. Learning the laws regulating fishing and avoiding egg-laden female lobsters, for example, are useful lessons to learn. The young fishermen become very respectful of their catch, only taking what they know will be consumed that evening.

The fish is cleaned and eaten straight after catching. Turks islander, Fred, filets a large dorado

Spearing the fast-moving Spanish mackerel is a prize for any fisherman

Fish, conch and lobster are the main sources of protein on expedition. Main picture: Conch are retrieved from sea grass beds where these creatures graze.
Above left: The record-sized lobster taken from the reef fed 20 people. Above right: Two dolphin fish caught on lines during a deep water passage.

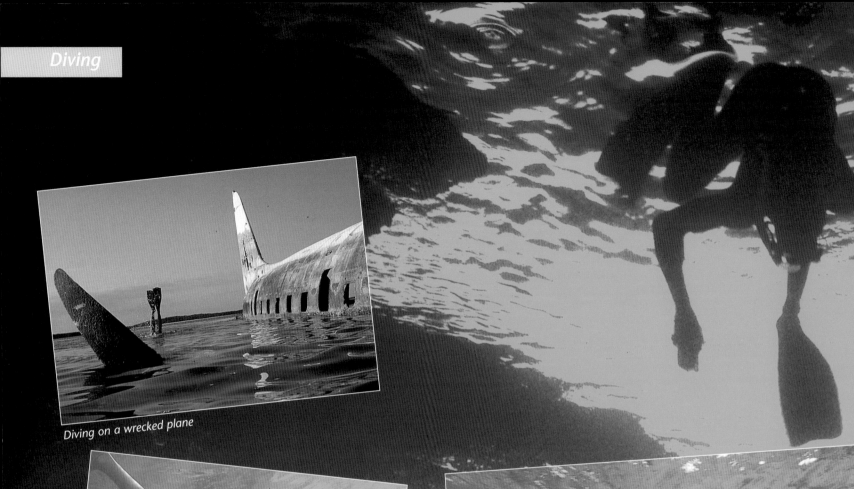

Diving on a wrecked plane

Diving is a daily activity on expedition. Julitika from Poland hovers over reef-building corals

Jane from England keeps an eye on a barracuda as it patrols the reef

Preparing for a night dive

Snorkelling is very much a part of daily life on expedition. After lunch there are often underwater explorations. Depending on the location these could involve swimming with dolphins, studying reef life or even catching a glimpse of a magnificent humpback whale. Scuba equipment is kept aboard the expedition boats and occasionally used, but only under strict control. Generally there is such a lot to see snorkelling that the extra risks involved in the use of scuba do not warrant its use with inexperienced teenagers.

Often, students are directed to areas of degradation to experience for themselves the effect of human impact on the health of marine environments.

IN THE SEEMINGLY PRISTINE clear waters of The Bahamas and Caribbean, pollution unfortunately does exist. The most noticeable type of pollution comes in the form of marine debris which lies in vast mounds along the windward shores of many islands. During expeditions young students and adults are exposed to marine debris through beach clean-ups. Using data cards from the Center for Marine Conservation, the team notes the variety of garbage found on remote beaches. Detailed analysis can determine the culprits. For example, large quantities of items bearing the logo of a particular cruise line can easily be traced back to the source. Just the process of picking up garbage, separating it and identifying it makes the students that much more aware of the problems our land and oceans face from man's negligence. The following selection of quotes written by students give a good example of how they are able to learn from their experience.

Balls of tar washed ashore on a deserted windward coast

During our one week in Big Sand Cay we did a beach clean-up and we found some amazing things. For the first time in my life, I realized the state of the earth. We just cleaned a section of the beach and we could find so many things; we collected 700 glass bottles, 500 plastic bottles, 4 wheels, navy stuff, plastic bags, rubber, wooden pallets and much more. If we don't find a solution to stop producing so much garbage the earth will be condemned to a big big dump.

REMI THEVENART, AGED 16, FRANCE

In an attempt to determine the amount and composition of this undesirable immigrant to our shores, Island Expedition is working with The Center for Marine Conservation to document this debris through beach clean-ups at each of the anchorages. Our findings so far reveal an unfortunate, but expected conclusion. Most of the garbage dumped in our waters is not generated by the people of The Bahamas and Caribbean, but by visitors. Furthermore, after combing the beaches, one can begin to speculate as to the origin of some of these sea-borne immigrants.

ERIN LOWE, TEACHER, THE BAHAMAS

Alberto from Haiti counting light bulbs

The fishing nets [drift nets] do not break down and fish, turtles and other animals can get caught in them. One net can kill hundreds of fish. Another thing you see are bottles. They do not do any harm to the wildlife but they decrease the aesthetic quality. The solution for plastics is recycling and reducing the amount of plastic that we buy.

AMANDA BRIGHTBILL, AGED 15, USA

Amanda Brightbill

Island Expedition
students analysing
marine debris
on remote islands

STUDENTS are given instruction in the use of underwater and topside 35 mm cameras and video equipment. They have an opportunity to create a photographic and written portfolio of their experiences which they often find very useful when presenting their expedition back at home. Many of the students have had their photographs published in magazines and some have had extracts of video footage included in films. The skills learned directly in the field can be a starting point for a career in media.

Dragan (left) filming; Alister from Grenada and Medi from France interviewing Dominican fisherman on the Silver Bank (see page 54)

Amandine from France photographing birds in a mangrove forest

Filming dolphin behaviour and vocalization (see page 101)

Felix from Fiji recording life on a coral reef (see pages 42–63)

Danah from the United States interviewing an elderly islander

GOOD COMMUNICATIONS are essential to a successful expedition. It is not hard to imagine the stress of being thrown together with people from every corner of the world, with a vast and varied range of experiences, opinions and ways of doing things. From the start, individuals have to be able to get on. Many adults might be horrified at the prospect of living in extremely close proximity with complete strangers, but the teenagers are usually more flexible than the adults.

The most exciting and rewarding aspect of the expedition ethos is the exchange of cultural and social perspectives. Friendships blossom despite the lack of a common language and one often witnesses conversations in a mixture of French, Spanish and English carrying on quite naturally.

A more formal language programme, which

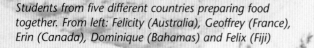

Students from five different countries preparing food together. From left: Felicity (Australia), Geoffrey (France), Erin (Canada), Dominique (Bahamas) and Felix (Fiji)

complements the natural exchanges of this multicultural environment, covers the basics of grammar and vocabulary. Students compile a daily list of relevant words which are translated into French, English and Spanish and noted in the daily expedition log book. The School at Sea has a library on board with a range of texts, novels and dictionaries in several languages.

A unique fact of the School at Sea is that it seeks to enrol children from across social boundaries. For example, the team may include well-travelled, highly educated European and North American children as well as orphans from Third World countries. The potential for learning is boundless; the more privileged children are in awe of the practical skills the less fortunate individuals are often able to teach them. Likewise, the less educated, many of whom lack basic writing skills, are thankful for help when trying to put pen to paper.

Easter Sunday celebrated in an abandoned coconut grove making Easter bonnets

Method

Ingredients

Americans
Australians
Bahamians
French
One Italian
Canadians
One Spaniard
One Belgian
One German
One Swede
One Fijian
One Dane

Utensils

Caribbean Islands
Cottage
Sailboats
Shipwreck
Reefs
Hammocks

Step 1 Take a handful of excited Australians and mix them with three teaspoons of French and one tablespoon of Italian in a cottage in Nassau.

Step 2 Gradually add some young Bahamians, three spicy Americans, two fresh Canadian girls and one ripe Spanish male.

Step 3 This dish must be served HOT, so add one sweet student from Belgium, a Fijian prince, a German doctor, a Swedish blond and a couple of Popovs.

Step 4 Have a fundraising party and bring it to the boil.

Step 5 While people are still hot, place in two prepared sailboats with a Danish crew on the side to form an expedition.

Step 6 Sail carefully through The Bahamas, dive on reefs and learn to mix with island people. Camp on beaches and sunbake until brown.

Step 7 Sail overnight to the Turks and Caicos and keep adding adventures and handfuls of good times, stirring in a swim with a friendly dolphin.

Step 8 Simmer as a team for a month and then place on a rusty shipwreck surrounded by whales. String up some hammocks and swing at night for two weeks.

Step 9 Share a lifetime of experiences and memories. Cook without prejudice and share cultural differences. Learn each other's languages and expand your knowledge. After three months the mixture should be stiff and stuck hard together. Cut into slices and one by one send back to various countries well done and filled with fresh memories never to fade.

DANA WHITE, AGED 15, AUSTRALIA

Dana White from Australia (left) with some of her expedition friends: Marie (Belgium), Amanda (USA) and Milan (The Bahamas)

Orphan Miguel from Chile not only shared his traditional Chilean folklore but taught other children practical skills he had learned out of necessity

Marine Ecosystems

B Y FAR THE MOST FASCINATING ECOSYSTEM in The Bahamas and Caribbean is the coral reef. Here, thousands of species belonging to practically all known phyla coexist in a competitive but successful balance. From the zooxanthellae algae living symbiotically within the coral polyp, to the carnivorous groupers preying on grunts, all individuals are in some indirect or direct way dependent on all others in a complex food chain. To understand this is to realize the need to preserve the cycle of life involved in nature's cities – the reefs.

The majority of marine species found throughout the world's tropical zone are concentrated around the reef. Species abundance measured per square metre shows that coral reefs are more productive than any other ecosystem worldwide, more than a rain forest and much more than a cornfield. Yet if you were to combine all the coral reefs of the world they would only cover an area the size of Venezuela. Despite this, they host one-quarter of all marine species known.

The reef-building corals form the base of an extremely productive ecosystem and food chain. Forms of algae, sponges, hydroids, tunicates, bryozoans and tube worms attach themselves to the protected rocks and reef. Stone crabs, spiny lobster and moray eels seek protection in holes and crevices. A kaleidoscope of fish live in and around the reef for the majority of their lives, always wary of larger predators such as groupers, barracuda, mackerel or sharks.

Fish of every imaginable colour and size in the coral reefs of The Bahamas

THE REEF-BUILDING or hermatypic coral acts as a mason for nature's underwater cities, continuously building the foundations of the reef, which, like any city, houses many different life forms.

Corals belong to the phylum Cnidaria which also includes the hydras, jellyfish and sea anemones. Consequently, corals share many of their features. The brilliantly coloured tentacles arranged like a flower in radial symmetry give them a delicate beauty of their own. At night corals stretch out their small tentacles to capture small planktonic animals. Within the tentacles a discharge of thin venomous filaments called nematocysts entangle and paralyse the prey. They also entrap their food using mucus.

A living coral polyp, a few millimetres in width, thrives inside a cup-shaped calcium carbonate skeleton. Around the polyp are thousands of other colonial polyps that form a latticework of grooves and compartments. In the case of the brain coral (*Diploria* sp.), the formation of the limestone body has a shape similar to a human cerebrum. The living portion of the coral, the thin top covering of the large boulder-like coral, is responsible for calcium carbonate production.

Reef-building can only be achieved through a fascinating and complicated symbiotic relationship between the animal polyp, and unicellular algae called zooxanthellae. The zooxanthella plant lives directly in the tissue of the polyp and like any other plant or alga uses photosynthesis for food production. A significant portion of the carbon that the zooxanthellae fix during photosynthesis is taken up by the coral. The nutritive needs of the coral are obtained from the planktonic animals it feeds on and whose waste products becomes available to the plant in the form of nitrogen and phosphorus. The coral provides the plant with food and shelter and the plant provides the coral with food, but how does this symbiotic relationship facilitate the deposition of a calcium carbonate skeleton? Corals absorb calcium ions from sea water. They are combined with carbon dioxide (CO_2) and water (H_2O) to form a soluble $Ca(HCO_3)_2$. The zooxanthellae algae remove the CO_2 and this forms insoluble calcium carbonate ($CaCO_3$) which the coral uses to build its skeleton.

A colony of star coral tentacles stretch out at night to trap food

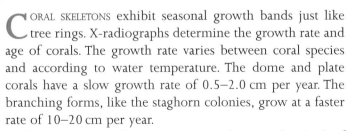

ORAL SKELETONS exhibit seasonal growth bands just like tree rings. X-radiographs determine the growth rate and age of corals. The growth rate varies between coral species and according to water temperature. The dome and plate corals have a slow growth rate of 0.5–2.0 cm per year. The branching forms, like the staghorn colonies, grow at a faster rate of 10–20 cm per year.

Experiments in the lab where corals were deprived of their symbiotic plant or placed in the dark showed considerably slower growth. There are over 60 genera of corals that hosts zooxanthellae. Deep-water corals and colder water corals lack zooxanthellae, but all reef-building corals possess them.

As has been mentioned, temperature plays an important role in coral growth. Comparative studies done in Jamaica and Bermuda reveal that the *Diploria* of Jamaica grew considerably faster than the ones in the cooler waters of Bermuda. Very low or very high temperatures can also affect corals. Natural disease called bleaching occurs when the zooxanthellae algae expel themselves from the host. This can be prompted by extremes of temperature such as those generated by El Niño or by unusually cold weather.

CORALS ARE HERMAPHRODITES that reproduce asexually and sexually. During a specific moon phase many coral species mass spawn. The corals release millions of eggs and sperm into the water. The sexually fertilized egg of a coral polyp becomes a planktonic disc-shaped larva called a planula. Once it attaches to a vacant space on the hard substrate it will remain sessile and become the parent to the whole colony by asexual reproduction or budding. This division of cells to produce new clones in the colony can last for hundreds of years, producing the large coral formations.

Another common type of asexual reproduction in branching corals is by fragmentation. When broken pieces of staghorn coral (*Acropora cerviconis*) fall on a suitable substrate they may begin growing and produce a new colony.

The spiny lobster is by far the most highly prized commercial resource. It scavenges on the reef at night and spends most of the day hidden in coral crevices

A white-spotted tilefish

The Caribbean reef shark, highest on the food chain, cruises the reef in search of food

The queen angel fish displays its vibrant colours

Reef structure

Tᴴᴱʀᴇ ᴀʀᴇ ꜰᴏᴜʀ ᴄᴀᴛᴇɢᴏʀɪᴇs of reefs found in The Bahamas and Caribbean. They are the barrier reefs, fringing reefs, bank or patch reefs and atolls.

Barrier Reefs

Barrier reefs are formed either parallel to a coastline or extend out on the shallow bank. Barrier reefs close to land are separated from the land by a lagoon and, at their shallowest part, the corals will break the surface at low tide. The barrier reefs off Belize and Andros in The Bahamas are, respectively, the second and third largest in the world after the Australian Barrier Reef.

A small section of a barrier reef

Fringing reefs

Fringing reefs are considered some of the youngest coral reefs. The fringing reefs extend outwards from the coastline and are sometimes separated from the land by a lagoon. Often confused with barrier reefs, the lagoons in fringing reefs are shallower and relatively close to the land.

Bank or patch reefs

Bank or patch reefs are circular or irregular reefs that form half a mile or more from shore or inside the lagoons of barrier reefs and atolls. On the extensive shallow water areas of The Bahamas, bank reefs are often called heads. Most texts describe bank reefs as small reefs but this is not always the case. The enormous heads in the deeper Silver Bank and in the Turks and Caicos reach to the surface from up to 20 metres down.

Atolls

Atolls are most often formed when volcanic islands sink due to subsidence of the sea floor, leaving the growing reef with a lagoon in the middle. When the land sinks the reef type changes from a fringing into a barrier reef. Atoll reefs are a common phenomenon in the Pacific Ocean, but very rare in the Atlantic Ocean. Hogsty Reef in the southern Bahamas is an example of one of only two atolls in the Atlantic. In the Caribbean Sea there are atolls along the Belize and Honduras coast.

Bank or patch reef

49

THE DIFFERENT TYPES OF CORAL include: the branching staghorn, elkhorn and finger colonies, the large star, brain and boulder corals, the plate-like group, the fuzzy pillar corals and all the encrusting, solitary and soft corals.

In a reef system, coral types inhabit different zones according to their specific light requirements and tolerance to wave motion. The encrusting and branching forms will generally be found at the top while the plate-like and larger colonies are below, away from the breakers.

Gorgonians or soft corals include the sea whips, sea feathers, sea fans and the red corals which have all been overexploited because of their bright colours and plant-like appearance. The gorgonians get their name from the organic substance called gorgonin that is found throughout the rod-shaped body of the animal.

Gorgonians or soft corals are often visited by trumpet fish and others which mimic their form

Star or boulder corals are the largest types of coral found on the reef

Staghorn coral provides protection for smaller fish such as these blue chromis

Finger corals feeding

CORAL REEFS are the essential breath for a vast and still little-known marine life. The zooxanthellae unicellular algae which live in the animal's polyp provide the essential oxygen for the coral to live and proliferate. Without the algae the reef would not grow and without the coral a score of marine organisms would not exist. Major marine resources – the spiny lobster (locally called crawfish), groupers, snappers, jacks, grunts and even the conch – exist because of the coral reefs and their associated environments such as mangroves. When coral reefs are destroyed, the algae and corals are killed. When you destroy the coral you strangle the marine life and deprive our future children of nourishment from the sea.

It is dismal to see the many destructive effects man has on the coral reef environment. Activities such as the use of chlorine bleach or other chemicals for removing exploited marine species, the dumping of waste and garbage, the unsustainable development of land, dredging, the throwing of anchors directly on the coral, the taking and breaking of corals by careless divers are some of the serious dangers to the reef and its inhabitants.

The expedition extensively documented fishing methods in The Bahamas and Caribbean and found that overfishing and overly efficient methods of fishing are having a great impact on coral reef ecosystems and fish stocks.

Research carried out on the Silver Bank (page 54) illustrates how poor fishing methods are slowly but surely degrading the biodiversity of an extensive coral reef system in the Caribbean. It is important to note that a number of the larger islands in the Caribbean such as Hispaniola (Dominican Republic and Haiti), Cuba, Puerto Rico and Jamaica have practically fished out their waters. In desperation, fishermen are venturing further out and sometimes poaching illegally in areas of more abundance like The Bahamas.

Overly efficient methods of fishing are having a detrimental effect on coral reefs and their commercially valuable inhabitants. The use of chlorine bleach by commercial divers has decimated entire coral reef systems

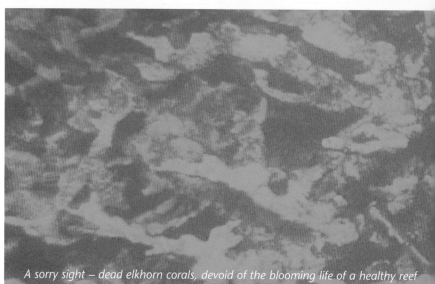

A sorry sight – dead elkhorn corals, devoid of the blooming life of a healthy reef

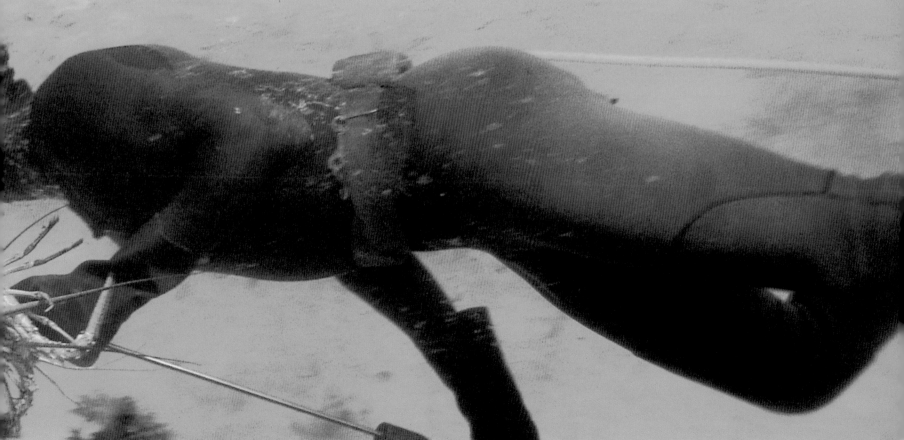

SIXTY MILES OFF THE NORTH COAST of the Dominican Republic, the 450 square mile area of the Silver Bank is predominantly a reef environment. There is an almost continuous breaking coral reef extending from the southeastern point to the northwestern point of the bank. Large coral towers rise from as deep as 23 metres to the surface on the interior of the bank. Compared to other reefs in The Bahamas and Caribbean, the Silver Bank has a much greater abundance of coral reefs per square mile and is deeper overall.

Unfortunately the majority of the reef-building corals inspected by the expedition are dead or dying, hence there is not the diversity of invertebrates and fish life that you find in healthy growing reefs. Over 10 years of annual surveying, Island Expedition has seen a slow decline in marine life.

The expedition interviewed the fishermen and observed their fishing methods. Fishing operations from the Dominican Republic, consisting of mother ships carrying on board 10–16 working skiffs, sweep through the Silver Bank each year. Two- or three-man teams, on the small skiffs powered by 15 h.p. outboard engines, use spear-guns and 'hookay gear' (underwater breathing apparatus) to gather spiny lobsters, fish and conch from the coral reefs.

There have been no ongoing scientific studies done on the Silver Bank that attempt to determine why the reefs are not healthy. The steady decline of biodiversity in the coral reef habitats of the Silver Bank could be due to a combination of hurricanes, overfishing and destructive methods of fishing.

Hopefully, the observations and reef surveys the expedition has already done on the Silver Bank, will interest scientists, experts and government officials to analyse seriously the problem with coral reef degradation in this incredibly dense coral reef area.

Per square mile the Silver Bank has a far greater density of corals than many other bank systems in the Caribbean. Sadly, the combination of overfishing and exposure to hurricanes has led to a degradation in biodiversity

● **Overly Efficient Fishing Methods**
Chlorine bleach, detergents and
cyanide are used to capture inaccessible
fish and spiny lobsters. These powerful
chemicals will instantly kill corals, algae
and other small invertebrate life which in
turn destroys the ecosystem of the reef.
Also the use of explosives kills a variety of
small and non-commercial fish.

The recent use of traps on longline
gear, dropped and occasionally dragged
on the ocean floor, is currently wiping out
entire populations of groupers and snappers
and destroying coral colonies.

*Spearing groupers with the aid of compressors is
particularly destructive to populations during their
winter spawning aggregations*

The Plight of the Nassau Grouper

The Nassau grouper (*Epinephelus striatus*) is a solitary fish that is high up on the food chain among reef dwellers. During its reproductive phase in the winter it aggregates by the thousands in particular spawning sites. For generations fishermen used traditional methods of catching the grouper using lines and traps (pots). Recently, spearfishing with compressors is used to catch groupers during the mating season. Disturbing the fertile groupers during this short and crucial period of reproduction will decimate the large grouper populations of The Bahamas.

Many Caribbean countries have already lost their groupers to similarly short-sighted methods of fishing. One solution to ensure Nassau grouper stocks for the future would be to establish 'no-take' marine reserves in those sites where they aggregate in large numbers for reproduction. Through the efforts of BREEF (Bahamas Reef Environment Educational Foundation), the Fisheries Department of The Bahamas and Island Expedition, several 'no-take' marine reserves have been considered in The Bahamas.

Fishermen employing traditional trapping methods cannot expect the returns of their modern and reckless counterparts

- **Unsustainable Development**
Silt from construction, development and deforestation smothers the reefs.

Destruction of the Land Affects the Sea
On Halls Pond Cay in The Bahamas, ironically in the heart of a land and marine reserve, a foreign owner cut over 20 miles of two lane size tracks on an island hardly two miles long. Small islands cannot tolerate changes to the extent that larger islands can; the balance of life on these fragile islands is extremely sensitive. Uncontrolled stripping of vegetation leads to sediments washing into the nearby coral reefs and other marine ecosystems. During heavy downpours, the enormous roads act like rivers, washing lose debris and soil into the surrounding waters. The silt is taken by the currents and smothers the coral reef and carries excess fresh water which the environment is not accustomed to in such quantities.

Island Expedition raised so much public attention concerning the devastation at Halls Pond Cay that the Bahamian Prime Minister, the Hon. Hubert Ingraham, went to visit the small private island to put a stop to any further development and ordered the owner to repair the damage.

Unsustainable development of land can have a great impact on nearby reefs (see photo on page 59)

Reckless Boating and Diving
Broken coral, caused by careless snorkellers and SCUBA divers, becomes extremely vulnerable to infectious disease from blue-green algae and bacteria and often dies. Throwing anchors from boats on the reef breaks the coral and leads to similar infections. Boaters tossing garbage and plastic bags overboard diminish the aesthetic value of the reefs and the plastic bags wrap themselves around the corals literally strangling them.

Buoys safeguard the coral reefs from boat anchors

- **Human Waste, Fertilizers and Pesticides**

  Run-off from agricultural fertilizers and sewage dumped into coastal waters creates rapid algal growth which strangles the reef. Pesticides used to eliminate mosquitoes end up in the ocean. The worst are the larvicides that are placed in ponds to kill off mosquito larvae. If these leach into the sea they will also kill coral and reef creatures in their larval form.

A once healthy coastal or fringing reef has been destroyed by run-off caused by unsustainable stripping of land vegetation

- **Coast Protector**
  Many of the coral reefs form a barrier on the windward and exposed side of islands. These reefs protect the low-lying coastline from ocean waves and stormy weather.

- **Beaches**
  The skeletal remains of corals, molluscs, coralline algae and tube worms consist of calcium carbonate that breaks down into sand which helps form our lovely beaches.

- **Food**
  A number of species harvested by commercial fishermen live on the reef or use the reef as a food source.

- **Tourism**
  The beauty of the reefs attract divers from all over the world. This generates tourism revenue for many countries.

- **Research and Medicine**
  The reefs serve as a living lab for scientists and students. Among the incredible diversity of animals and plants on the reef are organisms which produce unique chemicals that are used in medical research.

(a)

Benefits of coral reefs: (a) coast protection; (b) beaches; (c) food; (d) tourism; (e) research and medicine

THE BAHAMAS and Caribbean islands depend mainly on the sea for their tourism and fishing. The fishing industry is under threat; overly efficient methods are wiping out traditional fishing grounds. The introduction of more 100 per cent 'no-take' marine reserves is one 'insurance policy' to safeguard our fish stocks.

It has already been observed that the 'no-take' marine reserves in several Caribbean countries and south Florida have great benefits in replenishing marine resources or at least in some cases they diminish the degradation factor. Water moves constantly, carrying eggs and larvae away from their place of origin. Crawfish, conch and fish, having reached a good size in the protected reserve environment, move out of the 'no-take' zone to provide a good catch for local fishermen.

Being a stable environment, the 'no-take' zone has allowed for more accurate research on fish, shellfish and conch distribution and production. Ongoing research on the principal fishing resources has shown that the value of protecting conch in a 22 by 8 mile area (the Exuma Land and Sea Park) provides the fishing industry with several million dollars each year. The park is a nursery ground for baby conch. Left to grow as nature intended, adult conch migrate out of the park boundaries and provide a living for fishermen. The mature conch that remain in the park produce larvae which drift in the water to establish themselves way beyond their place of birth. One can think of the 'no-take' marine reserve as a restocking zone – not just for conch but also for grouper, lobster and all forms of commercially valuable fish. Both directly and indirectly, each marine reserve, if managed properly, can bring millions of dollars to the islands' economies.

Experts around the world explain that the location and types of areas pinpointed as marine reserves are very important and that the reserves have to be monitored by wardens as well as by nearby community members. Land adjoining marine reserves also needs to be protected from unsustainable development.

The implementation of more land and marine reserves in The Bahamas and the Caribbean is a vital step for the future of the sea and man's dependence on it. 'No-take' marine reserves are not only a theory but also a solution.

It takes thousands of years to build a reef structure like this one on the coral wall of Hogsty Reef

Mangrove Forests

T HE RED MANGROVE (*Rhizophora mangle*) forests of The Bahamas and Caribbean islands are frequently overlooked, yet they are extremely important in a number of functions benefiting both the shoreline and sea environment. These short and sturdy trees with their elegant limbs rooted firmly underwater reduce the water flow across the shoreline and augment sedimentation on land. They also represent a nursery ground for a variety of marine species, as well as a number of birds.

Red mangrove forests are extremely beneficial to islands and their surrounding life. They prevent erosion of land, act as a nursery ground to many marine creatures and attract a number of birds like these plovers

SURPASSED only by the reef environment, the red mangroves abound in biological activity. It can hardly be suspected until sneaking up upon the tangled golden-red roots. Inside the meshwork of roots live an assortment of grunts, schoolmasters, grey snappers and occasionally a congregation of juvenile spiny lobster. Juvenile Nassau groupers are well camouflaged among the roots and escape their many predators thus hidden. There are usually scores of other marine plants and unexploited species of animals that inhabit the red mangroves, with many of them adapted to live at specific levels in the tidal zone. Snails, limpets, barnacles, oysters, tunicates, sponges, sabellid worms, shrimps, crabs, jellyfish are some of the invertebrates that attach to the roots.

Perfectly adapted to the harsh salt-water environment, red mangroves root themselves firmly in shallow coastal waters and creeks

ABOVE THE WATER line the foliage is a haven for mosquitoes. Their larvae, if not eaten by fish, will be born in the quiet water inside the mangroves. Birds will come to feast on the mosquitoes and some establish nests in the branches. For example the mangrove coppice located in the shallow waters of the Turks and Caicos provides a nesting ground for a most impressive colony of frigate birds, often known as man-o'-war birds.

Mangrove forests are closely linked to the coral reefs. Numerous animals that feed on the reef are, in their juvenile form, thriving in the mangroves. When you close off mangrove creeks or destroy them through development projects, the number of animals found on the nearby reefs diminishes over time.

The magnificent frigate bird nests and raises its young in the protection of this mangrove bush

THE RED MANGROVE'S ability to reclaim the land and live in a saltwater environment has made it a leader in the ecological sequence called succession. Succession refers to the different steps necessary for plants and animals to establish a climax community in a particular type of environment. The climax community is a balanced and stable ecosystem – the final product in the sequence of events of succession. For the red mangroves this process begins with the release of the seedling in the water. Land plants usually invest a lot of energy in producing massive amounts of seeds in the hope that a few will settle in the right environment and sprout. The mangrove, on the other hand, does not release the seedling until the fruit is almost 30 cm long. The long and narrow fruit is so well adapted to survival in salt water that it can float for up to one year in this harsh environment. Once it settles it will penetrate the sand and root itself. Leaves will grow profusely and the development of prop roots which curve and extend into the water will begin. Leaves will steadily fall off and settle on the bottom. The leaves are decomposed by bacteria and marine fungi and over a period of time this changes the consistency of the muddy sand to a richly packed sediment. Now that the soil is fertile, a nutritional cycle begins attracting algae, filter feeders, marine grazers and predators. A complete marine food chain is now established.

After years of accumulation of detrital material, the composition of the soil becomes anaerobic and the sediment build-up is slightly too high for the red mangrove to survive. This allows for the succession of the black mangrove (*Avicennia nitida*) which thrives in an area only periodically flooded by the tides. The black mangrove has developed specialized finger-like air breathing rootlets called pneumatophores to survive in this anoxic (oxygen free) environment. As the black mangrove grows and more leaves fall on the moist muddy soil, the consistency of the sediment changes again and succession continues. The next mangrove in line is the white mangrove (*Laguncularia racemosa*) which lives in a muddy saline ground. The white mangrove can be recognized by looking closely at the petiole or stem that supports the leaf where glands for removing excess salt exist. On slightly higher and drier saline soil dwells the last in the mangrove family, the buttonwood (*Conocarpus erecta*). The buttonwood represents the end of the ecological succession of mangroves and can generally be identified by its jade and silver coloured foliage.

One island that is ideal for the study of succession is Shroud Cay, located in the heart of the Exuma Land and Sea Park, Bahamas. Mangrove swamps cover 65 per cent of the island, which make it one of the larger in the chain of over two hundred Exuma cays. Several times a year Island Expedition and the School at Sea have explored Shroud Cay to show students the variety of mangroves and their different stages of development. There are areas where the recently rooted plants have a few virgin leaves poking up just above the high tide mark. Nearby are small mangrove bushes extending their prop roots as if they are marching on new land. Pencil-shaped black mangroves stand firm in rows in the dense sulphur-smelling mud, a sign of an anaerobic environment. White mangroves and buttonwoods grow just above the water's edge and show the clear-cut barrier between them and their waterlogged relatives.

The black mangroves are second in line in the succession of mangroves. Their pencil-shaped breathing tubes protrude from anaerobic mud

Types of mangrove forest

MANGROVE FORESTS are found throughout the Caribbean islands. The mangrove can thrive in very protected creeks or along shorelines. From surveys conducted in The Bahamas and Caribbean by Island Expedition it was noted that mangroves are much more common on the shallow and protected (leeward) coast of major islands. In contrast, on the windward side, which is often comprised of the rugged rocky shores and sandy beaches, there are only occasional small outcrops of mangroves. However, mangroves within creek systems can be found on both the windward and leeward sides of islands. The entrances to these mangrove creeks are generally very inconspicuous, but hide a labyrinth of winding mangrove rivers. Within the mangrove creeks are patches of sand banks, sea grass beds and small coral formations.

In several locations mangrove creeks lead into a perfect enclosure with a deep enough channel entrance for boats seeking shelter. One of the best is at Allans-Pensacola Cay in The Bahamas where a perfect natural hurricane harbour exists. Thickets of mangrove vegetation have formed along the narrow channel and inside the deeper peanut-shaped harbour.

Throughout the islands you will find endless tangles of mangrove forests that provide protection for a myriad of marine and land species. The high density of decaying leaf matter provides a nutrient-rich environment that is an essential base for the life cycle of many animals and plants. The firm grip the roots take on the land helps to prevent erosion caused by water currents and, hence, augments the boundaries of the land.

The constant flow of water at the mouth of any mangrove creeks is essential for proper nutrient exchange to maintain a flourishing mangrove community. Unfortunately many land developers do not see the benefits of mangroves and have already demolished far too many in the Caribbean and elsewhere in the world to build hotels, harbours and residential housing projects. Mangrove creek systems are particularly attractive to developers as they provide lucrative and naturally protected waterfront sites.

The red mangrove is adapted to a very harsh salty environment that has allowed it to survive for thousands of years without competition. Furthermore, the chemical tannin, which gives the mangroves their red colour, is also used by man as a tanning and dye agent. Potential enemies like marine borers and grazers find the bark and leaves of this chemically protected plant unpalatable. However, mangroves cannot tolerate pollutants. Pollution from towns, pesticides and insecticides and oil spills have a very adverse effect on the mangroves. Without proper management and care of this coastal vegetation, many life forms could lose their habitat.

It is essential that we take action to limit the destruction of mangroves. A mangrove replenishment initiative could be introduced and implemented in The Bahamas and the Caribbean islands. The purpose of the project would be to educate the public about the benefits of mangrove forests and to protect and restore forests which are under threat from development or pollution.

The tannin dye found in the roots of the red mangrove protects it from marine borers, but cannot save it from the impact of careless development and pollution

THE SANDY ENVIRONMENT is described by many as an underwater desert, barren and lifeless. Compared with the biologically rich reefs and mangroves this may seem true but these areas are far from inactive. They are home to the burrowing animals. When one sees a sand tilefish dive headfirst and disappear in its burrow, or when goatfish probe and scuffle the sand with chin barbels in search of food, one realizes there must be something of value in the sand. Small shrimps, crabs and worms inhabit this hidden world.

The vast area of shallow water between the coastal mangrove forest and coral reefs is composed mainly of sand banks and sea grass. The banks are constantly shifting, sometimes building up small islands of sand that are completely exposed, even during the highest tides. The sea grass areas are more stable because sea grass roots bind the sand securely to the ocean floor. These two types of environments are treated together because they are closely related. The sea floor can be exclusively sand, rooted with scattered sea grass or dense sea grass beds.

The widespread regions of sea grasses are mostly made up of turtle grass (*Thalassia*). It grows in dense beds on the ocean floor and provides food for many marine grazers. The green turtle, which gives turtle grass its name, will spend its adult life (it is carnivorous as a juvenile) grazing on acres of this plant. Numerous types of snails, especially the conch, feed on *Thalassia*. The bright pink shell of *Strombus gigas* is one of the largest in the world and the meat inside is a very important food item in The Bahamas and Caribbean. The conch uses its radula (mouth) to graze on the sea grass. The tulip shell, one of the most aggressive gastropods (marine snails), along with the hermit crab, a crustacean, are both predators of small conch. Hermit crabs start out living in small shells, and as they grow invade even larger mature conchs. The smaller milk conch and cushioned sea star live in close proximity on the grass flats.

Turtle grass carpets a good portion of the shallow Caribbean sea floor

THE NUTRITIONAL VALUE of the sea grass is enhanced by epiphytes and small animals and plants which grow on its blades. In shallow sand flats one will find small pipefish and sea horses camouflaged within the blades. Seahorses are predatory animals which wrap their prehensile tails around the grass and wait for a small crab to wander too close. One type of jellyfish is particularly at home in sea grass. Unlike most jellyfish which move with the current, *Cassiopeia xamachana* will generally stay on the sea grass bottom, tentacles upward, hence it is called the upside-down jellyfish. The gently pulsating jellyfish are generally most plentiful near or within mangrove creeks.

The primary dwellers of the sand and sea grass terrain are mostly invertebrates, including the sand dollars, sea cucumbers, sea biscuits, sea urchins and sea stars. All of these animals belong to the phylum Echinodermata, meaning 'spiny skin'. The common sand dollar and its close relative the sea biscuit are for the most part hidden in the sand when alive. The cushioned sea star (*Oreaster* sp.) is an important resident of these areas and can devour clams by enveloping the shell with its thousands of membranous tube feet which prise open the bivalve. It is important to note that sea stars are incorrectly called starfish. They have nothing to do with fish which are vertebrates.

The white sea urchin is also a common resident of turtle grass fields. The test (body) of this sea urchin can reach up to 18 cm across. The spines covering the whole test are very small, enabling the curious observer to pick up the animal and find underneath a cluster of sea grass blades which have been clipped and are ready to be munched.

Another important survivor of the sandy environment is the lugworm (*Arenicola cristata*). The lugworm digs U-shaped burrows in the sand found close to shore or in shallow stagnant waters. The worm is hard to find, but its presence is recognized by the large sand mounds it produces from the discarded sand it ingests. Another animal which vacuums tonnes of sand, extracting the necessary nutrients and spewing the rest from its excretory end, is the sea cucumber.

Worms and clams remain hidden under their sand mounds while their neighbours, the sea stars, are far more conspicuous

SPONGES ARE AMONG the few commercially valuable animals collected from sand and sea grass terrains. Sponging was at one time one of the main fishing industries. In the early 1930s a fungal disease killed off the majority of the sponges. Today, sponges are found in great numbers scattered throughout The Bahamas' banks and fishermen are beginning to harvest again. There are three exploited sponges – the grass, sea wool and silk sponge – each having particular properties that are attractive for the cosmetic industry. There are many other varieties of sponges, mostly found on the reefs, that are not commercially viable.

The soft sand is the ideal hiding place for the southern stingray (*Dasyatis americana*). This ancient cartilaginous fish is one of the larger vertebrates that uses the sand for both protection and feeding. Using its large pectoral fins, the stingray covers its body with sand, leaving its dark eyes exposed to scrutinize the area for sharks, its primary predator. The stingray will devour scores of juvenile conch by crushing the shell with its hard plate-like mouth.

The sandy bottom also harbours a source of food for marine mammals. The bottlenose and spotted dolphins use their echolocation to detect a variety of sand fish and crustaceans buried in the sand (see page 101).

The rare bat fish hovering about turtle grass

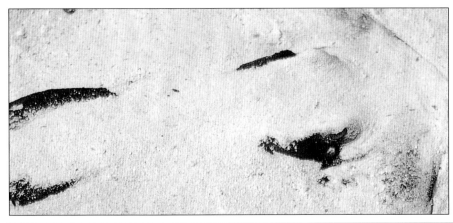

Barely visible, the southern stingray uses fine sand for camouflage as it hides from its main predator the shark

Students showing large conch shells in a shallow sand and sea grass terrain

Whales of the Silver Bank

Polyxeni: A Whale Observation Base

The isolated Silver Bank is the favoured wintering spot for the North Atlantic humpback whale which migrates to mate and give birth. The **Polyxeni** wreck, in the background, has served as a whale observation base for Island Expedition

POLYXENI, A WRECK permanently fixed on the treacherous reefs of the tropical region called the Silver Bank, has been a base for Island Expedition since 1990 to observe humpback whales during the winter seasons. The isolated Silver Bank is the favoured wintering spot for the North Atlantic humpback whale (*Megaptera novaeangliae*) which migrates there to mate and give birth. The majority of the recorded observations were made from the bow of the shipwreck *Polyxeni* which provided an excellent and unobtrusive way of learning more about humpback whale behaviour. Generally, most humpback whale research is conducted from inflatables or larger boats in which the animals must be chased.

Polyxeni is located 80 nautical miles off the northern coast of the Dominican Republic and approximately the same distance from the southern coast of Grand Turk in the Turks and Caicos islands. Stretching for nearly 30 miles along the eastern edge of the Silver Bank is a large barrier reef that has taken countless ships.

*The **Polyxeni**, a 100 metre freighter which was wrecked in 1982*

With nothing else exposed but tips of coral at low tide and the 100-metres-long *Polyxeni*, which was wrecked in 1982, the Silver Bank has earned an unfavourable reputation with cruising vessels. Probably one of the earliest disasters was a sixteenth-century cargo ship loaded with silver extracted from the mines of South America. The ship crashed on the reef and apparently the surviving crew used the valuable cargo to stack a platform of silver bars within the branches of elkhorn coral, hence the area was named the Silver Bank. Naturally, there is no evidence to confirm this tale which may have been passed on by pirates who stripped the loot from under the wet feet of these desperate men stranded in the middle of the ocean.

Island Expedition's first trip to the Silver Bank in February 1990 included an aerial survey of the area to determine the safest passages to the wreck through the coral-laden bank. Having spent five years using only inflatables for expeditions, camping at night and roughing it the island way, Island Expedition found the wreck ideal to live on and especially to observe the whales. Before the expedition established itself on the wreck, a thorough inspection of the vessel was made to determine its safety and stability. Access to certain areas was restricted.

Breakfast, lunch and dinner were cooked on board the **Polyxeni**. Some students found a practical way to avoid the smoke

THE FIRST YEAR WAS THE TOUGHEST but the following years were spent in much greater comfort. Extra water, fuel and food supplies were brought over and this allowed the team to survive on the *Polyxeni* for extended periods of time. Hammocks were strung in the main sleeping area located under the bow's deck and were essential as the wreck is tilted. A large supply of wood enabled the meals to be prepared on an open fire on the sheltered starboard side of the *Polyxeni*. A large plastic tarp, which served to collect rain water and to provide shade, was stretched across the dining area. Long square logs (part of *Polyxeni's* original cargo) were cut and placed around the cooking area so that 20 or more people could sit. Bread, pizzas and cakes were cooked in the ship's old oven, located in the stern of the wreck. Bakers wore diving masks to screen the smoke. Staples, canned vegetables and fruits were eaten with mostly conch and fish caught from the surrounding waters. Pancakes were made every Sunday morning for breakfast.

Wood was also used to strengthen weak areas of the wreck and to construct small desks to study on. A small generator supplied all the electricity necessary to light up the kitchen and sleeping area, for the use of power tools and to recharge the batteries for the video and laptop computer. Large, salvaged ropes were placed along an 8 metre section of the port side to serve as bumpers for inflatables coming to and going from the wreck.

With the wreck permanently tilted, hammocks are best for staying level, especially to study and sleep

THE GROUP WORKED on a regular schedule with a rotation system for daily chores. School took place every morning from 8 until 12, except on Sundays. Special classes in languages (French, English and Spanish) and ecology were offered three times a week after lunch and the group gathered once a week to review articles written by each member that week. A daily log of activities was kept by the people in charge that day. The general whale activity for the day and the three daily (7.00 a.m., noon and 4.00 p.m.) recordings from the observation point on the bow of the wreck were kept in the whale log.

From 1990 until 1998 Island Expedition teams varied each year from 8 to 20 people, including visiting journalists, scientists and film makers, who spent from 2 to 8 weeks sleeping, eating and observing whales from the wrecked vessel. (Coincidently, *Polyxeni* means 'many nations' in Greek and to date the old lady has hosted 36 nationalities who spent many hours watching whales from her bow.)

*The aft port side of the **Polyxeni** was low enough to allow supplies and people to board easily*

The Humpback Whale

CETACEANS are marine mammals that breath air and give birth to live young which suckle milk. The term cetacean describes both whales and dolphins. Worldwide, 77 species of cetaceans have been recognized of which 11 are baleen (Mysticeti) whales and 66 species are toothed whales (Odontoceti). The baleen whales have a large bony jaw that holds plates of fibres (baleen) which filter planktonic organisms such as the krill shrimp. The toothed whales grasp fish with their jaw and can use sonar to stun or kill their prey.

The rorqual whales of the family Balaenopteridae are the only baleen whales that migrate to The Bahamas and Caribbean. The rorqual whales have long ventral grooves that enable elastic tissues below the lower jaw to stretch when swallowing massive quantities of water. Three different types of rorquals have been sighted by Island Expedition: the humpback whales (*Megaptera novaeangliae*), the minke whale (*Balaenoptera acuturostrata*) and the blue whale (*Balaenoptera musculus*). The blue whale is the largest animal to have lived on earth and is seldom sighted in the Caribbean while the humpback whales are by far the most numerous rorquals to visit Caribbean waters.

Scientists believe that the majority of the entire North Atlantic population of humpback whales pass through the Silver Bank during the winter. As many as 3000 humpback whales could be gathered on the banks during peak times. The average adult length is 13 metres and their weight varies from 25 to 30 tonnes. Two very distinct characteristics which differentiate humpback whales from other rorquals are their long pectoral flippers, from which their name Megaptera (big wing) originates, and their unusual behaviour.

Humpback whales are considered to be the most impressive of the large baleen whales. On many occasions expedition members have been fortunate to see these huge animals jumping completely out of the water in what is called a breach. The resounding splash from a breach can be seen miles away, and the act of jumping is believed to be the greatest caloric investment of any animal. While courting, the males will also exhibit extraordinary acts of slapping their long white pectoral flippers and tail flukes. Recordings of over 30 consecutive tail slaps by the same individual are not uncommon during this period of courtship.

From atop the *Polyxeni* the expedition have observed competitive groups of males, or bulls, which not only try to impress the females with fin, tail and body acrobatics but will also utilize some of these activities to injure each other. During one outing on the inflatables a battle between bulls proved to be bloody. During the expeditions it was observed that bulls did not show any physical aggression towards females or mother/calf/escort groups.

Females, also called cows, have a one year gestation period which coincides with their yearly winter migration to this tropical region. Most experts have agreed that the majority of females do not give birth on consecutive years, but instead take a break between pregnancies. However, occasionally the expedition have observed pregnant mothers swimming with a one-year-old calf. Although other scientists have noted this, further studies will be needed to prove the true relationship of the pregnant cow and calf.

Mothers and calves are usually accompanied by another whale called the escort. For many years the escort was believed to be a female acting as companion or nanny, but studies show that many escorts are actually males. The escort is possibly waiting for a chance to reproduce with the mature female it follows. From underwater encounters with mothers and calves, Island Expedition members found that escorts are rarely protective towards the young calves and often stayed away from the pod and avoided swimmers.

Individual humpback whales have been identified by taking photographs of the underside of their tail. When the whale prepares for a dive (sound), it lifts the tail flukes out of the water allowing for a photo ID. The pattern of white and dark coloration on the ventral side of the tail distinguishes individuals. On the inflatables, photography of tails for identification purposes was not a principal objective for the team. In order to obtain a good number of photo IDs researchers must spend most of the day following and chasing the whales.

The long ventral grooves on the underside on this humpback
calf are a distinctive characteristic of the rorqual family

Humpback Songs

O NE OF THE MOST enchanting aspects of the humpback whale is its songs. It is believed that the males only sing during the mating season and that the songs are associated with courtship rituals, but no one is sure. The humpback's haunting songs may be heard miles away with a variety of pitches that can be heard through a boat's hull. On one of the trips to the Mouchoir Bank, located west of the Silver Bank, it became apparent to expedition members why sailors once feared these large sea creatures. The melancholic songs of humpbacks resounded clearly through the steel hulled sailboat while students listened in awe and silence. During outings in the inflatables, one of the most favoured pastimes for students was to dive to 3 metres or more, close their eyes and listen to the mysterious songs of the humpbacks.

Robert and Katherine Payne, who pioneered the recording of humpback whale songs, discovered that the vocalization of humpbacks contained very specific and complex patterns. The Paynes and other sound experts believe that before the interference of engine noises on the sea, baleen whales may have been able to communicate over thousands of miles.

Oddly enough, the whales do not eat during their winter stay in the Caribbean waters. Unlike the nutrient-rich waters of the North Atlantic, these tropical waters lack the necessary planktonic food for the filter-feeding baleen whales. During the spring and summer in the northeastern part of North America and Arctic regions, the whales eat massive quantities of the small shrimp-like krill and accumulate a thick layer of blubber that insulates them from the cold water and fuels their lengthy migrations during the winter season.

The worldwide population of humpback whales, once numbering well over 100,000, was reduced to a few thousand individuals. In 1996 the International Whaling Commission finally banned commercial killing. Today the humpback whale is making a comeback and has rebounded, unlike other great whales, to approximately 25,000 individuals worldwide. With a continued international moratorium, research and education there can be hope for the continued survival of this fascinating and highly social marine mammal.

Timo and Sam listening to the enchanting
songs of the humpback whale

Whale Observations from the Wreck

THE BEAUTY of using the *Polyxeni* wreck as an observation point was that it did not move, did not make any noise and the whales never knew you were watching them. Another bonus was the *Polyxeni's* position; the bow perched on coral 12 metres above the water offered a spectacular 360 degree bird's eye view of the whales' activities, allowing for broad and accurate long range sightings. From the rusted rails of the bow, three times a day (7 a.m., noon and 4 p.m.), observations of whale activity were recorded over a 45 minute period. With binoculars glued to their eyes students and adults began observations to the South and every 5 minutes moved clockwise 45 degrees to the next sector, i.e. South West, West, and so on until they finished looking in the South again. When whales were sighted the note keeper wrote the time, distance, direction, cruising direction, approximate numbers, type of behaviour and any additional observations.

Apart from cruising and blowing, the most common activity recorded was tail slapping. The highest recorded number of consecutive tail slaps by one individual was 58. The slapping of their large pectoral flippers was also a common behaviour. Their jumps out of the water were often noted and sometimes they would perform this action tail first, in what is called a tail breach.

In order to make sure the same whale was not recorded more than once, the team tracked the whale movements with and without binoculars and stayed for only 5 minutes in each 45 degree sector. The whales closest to the observation point were monitored continually.

Tail slapping – members observed as many as 58 consecutive slaps

From the bow of the **Polyxeni** wreck, Island Expedition has recorded over 5000 observations of humpback whale behaviour

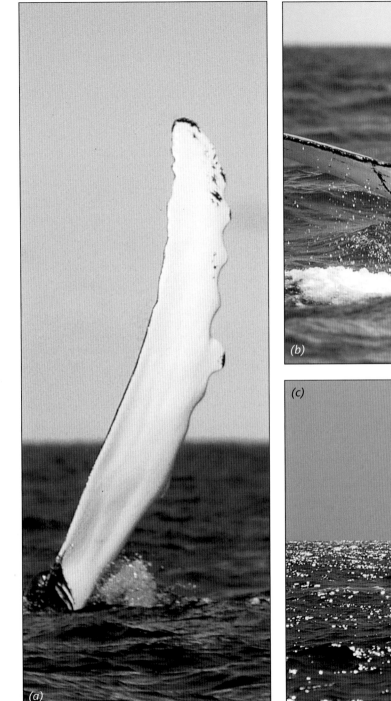

Typical humpback behaviours: (a) fin slapping – Megaptera, the humpback's scientific name, means big wing; (b) sounding – the ventral side of the whale's tail is the whale equivalent of a thumb print; (c) breaching – a spectacular show of strength

Whale Observations at Sea

Sixteen-year-old Adrian from Canada had this to say about his first encounter with a humpback:

'I swam past a beautiful coral head and saw a warm glow in the water ahead. As I swam closer, my heart pounding, I could see a graceful 40 foot humpback with her baby swimming at the surface. I looked below and also saw her escort. They turned in a circle towards me as if to say hello and then she gently touched my arm with her fin. Her eyes were as big as softballs and I could see every little line and mark on their bodies. I will never forget this day.'

For any avid diver, one of the most memorable experiences is to have swum alongside a large whale in crystal water. However, underwater encounters with whales are rare events which only a few lucky people have known. Whales, unlike their smaller cousins the dolphins, are less playful and are generally wary of boats and people, especially during the mating season. Observers along the eastern seaboard of the United States often have far longer encounters with humpbacks since they are calmer during their months of feeding. In most cases an underwater encounter in their southerly breeding grounds lasts only a few seconds to a few minutes.

Over the years the primary objective for underwater observation was to find better ways of approaching the whales unobtrusively. In most cases it involved just waiting patiently for the whales to come to the boat. This sometimes demanded much more time, but the rewards were much greater when the whales approached the inflatables or swimmers out of curiosity.

If a group of whales was sighted and had not sounded upon the boat's arrival, they were slowly followed with a steady speed which has proven to be a more effective method than constantly changing speed and trying to get in front of the whales. As divers slowly entered the water, the cautious rorquals kept their coconut-sized eyes fixed on the swimmers. A few times a snorkler was lucky enough to have the whale stay very close by, but as soon as the swimmer touched the whale, it immediately left. Fourteen-year-old Bruce Sidwell, a student on expedition, exemplifies this:

'I was just drifting in the water, occasionally diving under to listen to the whale's songs when into the blue I faintly saw a whale's white flippers fading in the distance. All of a sudden the whale changed direction and came towards me and even started to follow me, then it slowly raised out of the water and looked at me. All I could see was its large dark eye and I was trying to take a picture and say WOW at the same time. At one point it was so close I couldn't help touching it. It then quickly disappeared.'

Bruce's underwater experience was a good example of how the best encounters occurred when the team least expected them.

Findings

T HE MORE TIME one spends observing humpback whales, the more one realizes the complexity of their behaviour and how much is still unknown about them.

From the results of eight winters spent on the Silver Bank there seemed to be correlations between weather, time of year and presence of boats in the vicinity, and the number of whales and type of activity displayed. For example, it was noted that days with stronger winds showed more whale activity closer to the wreck and coral barriers and overall more breaching and splashing behaviour than cruising and sounding behaviour. On calmer days the splashing activity was less common, especially during hotter parts of the day. A number of mother,

calf and escort groups were observed resting in the shade of large coral heads during calm days.

It appeared that the presence of boats does not affect the number of whales in a particular area, but does affect whale behaviour. For instance, whales that splashed their tail, flipper or body on the water often stopped when the boats approached, or whales cruising at the surface sounded upon the boat's arrival.

The first two years that Island Expedition visited the Silver Bank there were only a few boats. Over the following years there has been a steady increase in the number of visitors, especially on live aboard dive boats. Today, the Silver Bank Whale Commission in Samana, Dominican

Republic has made the Silver Bank a sanctuary, requiring all boats staying for extended periods to obtain a permit and follow certain rules in whale watching.

Observations made by Island Expedition from the *Polyxeni* wreck and the reports it has presented have helped to set guidelines for whale watching on the Silver Bank. However, the expedition and other researchers are still very far from understanding the complex social behaviour of humpback whales. It will require many more years of observations to establish proper guidelines for whale watching, hoping, as time passes, that the whales can forgive the days of whale killing and approach humans with less fear.

The primary purpose of the whale project is educational. Daily observations allowed all participating students to understand more about humpback whale behaviour. Students who had never seen a live whale before became young experts. They also learned how to live efficiently in a very remote environment. They participated in a once in a lifetime journey studying whales from a wreck stranded in the middle of the Caribbean Sea.

Through its films, books and research expeditions, Island Expedition hopes to further enrich public knowledge of this most extraordinary marine mammal, the humpback whale.

At first I didn't quite realize what I was hearing. I took a deep breath and plunged straight down, heading for the sandy bottom far below. After popping my ears I heard a low deep moan, then another, then another, only higher pitched. It was a slow enchanting melody vibrating through the clear water. It was almost as if they were crying, the mellow sound coming straight from the soul. It pierced my heart, and from then on I was hypnotized – entranced by the whales.

We reached the edge of the pod in the inflatable, then slipped into the water quietly and swam around, waiting to see if the whales would come near us. Then through the water far below. I saw the white of a fin beginning to ascend from the misty depths. My heart began to beat fast. A large female swam straight past me. Following her was a curious calf who slowed down to swim at my pace. I forgot that I was underwater and inhaled.

I swallowed heaps of salty water and was running out of breath fast . . . I needed to empty the growing pool of water in my mask, but I did not want to miss this once in a lifetime chance.

With my heart beating so hard it almost popped through my skin I swam alongside this beautiful calf which was more than three times the size of me. I could see his hand-sized eye following my every move. Then the few seconds that seemed like hours ended and he left with his mother.

I surfaced and began screaming with excitement. For the rest of the day I had a smile from ear to ear that would not wipe off my face.

FROM 'ENCHANTING WHALES' BY FELICITY HORSLEY, AGE 15, AUSTRALIA

'The whale slowly turned directly towards me. All I could see was its large head with wings stretched out like a bird closing in on me very quickly'

'The whale, not the least bit afraid of my presence, started spinning using its long white pectoral fins to rotate its massive body over and over again'

'It displayed this behaviour for several minutes only a few metres away from me until it slowly rose to the surface. Words can never properly describe this very special encounter between whale and man'

I thought leaving the wreck was sad
because I had lived on it for two months
and finally I was leaving it.
I liked all my friends on the expedition.
Now they are all leaving and it's kind of sad.
I think I could write them but it has changed,
It will never be the same. I felt helpless.
Some people who don't know it might say:
'Yuk, this place looks like trash.'
But I would speak to them and say:
'This is my home you're talking about!'

FROM 'LEAVING THE WRECK',
BY STEVEN DARVILLE, AGED 13, THE BAHAMAS

Dolphins

SINCE ANTIQUITY there have been tales and legends describing the dolphin's altruistic behaviour towards man. Roman mosaics and coins dating from 500 BC show man playing with dolphins. In the eighteenth century Vietnamese sailors were rescued by a pod of dolphins after their naval vessel was sunk by Chinese invaders. Since then the Vietnamese people have worshiped dolphins and whales and erected a building called the Temple of the Whale.

It is not surprising that dolphins have become such a legendary part of religious and artistic culture. They are known to watch over travellers on the sea, and believed to help those who are leaving on an uncharted journey. Fishermen and sailors worldwide have told stories of dolphins warding off sharks or keeping people afloat so they can safely reach the shore.

A pod of dolphins

READING ABOUT HOW DOLPHINS have helped man however is not as convincing as actually experiencing it for yourself; as the saying goes 'seeing is believing'. It was on an expedition across the Great Bahama Bank to Bimini, when members of Island Expedition realized how interactive dolphins can be with humans. A team of four people were cruising on a 4.5 metre inflatable when suddenly a pod of bottlenose dolphins were sighted. The dolphins rode alongside the boat and surfed the bow wave, a common activity. After a few minutes the boat was stopped and the author entered the water to observe and photograph the dolphins. At first they were very calm, swimming close to the boat. After several minutes they began making a variety of high pitched whistles and grouped themselves together observing the author. Within a matter of a few seconds one of the dolphins, whistling incessantly, quickly moved away from the pod, nudging and circling the author. As the author followed the fast movement of the dolphin he saw a large tiger shark approaching. It is only in situations like this that humans suddenly develop an adrenaline boost that allows them to fly. The author immediately leaped out of the water and into the inflatable and the dolphins disappeared. Why did the dolphins not leave immediately when they realized a tiger shark, a predator of dolphins, was lurking around? Why did they attempt to communicate to the diver that danger was nearby? These are only a few of the questions that man has asked concerning dolphin behaviour which still remains very puzzling.

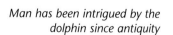

Man has been intrigued by the dolphin since antiquity

IKE MAN, DOLPHINS are warm blooded, air-breathing mammals, that mate and give birth to live young. The mothers feed milk to their young for some months and the young calf stays with the mother and other dolphins in the pod for years. Dolphins have one blow hole on top of their head and depending on the species, age and their physical exertion dolphins can stay submerged for up to 10 minutes

Dolphins are small toothed whales (Odontocetis) which, according to palaeontologists, evolved from land-based mammals that lived in brackish waters 55 million years ago. By 25 million years ago, the end of the Oligocene epoch, fossil records showed a variety of odontocetes.

The dolphin's smooth body enables it to streak through the water with great efficiency and speed. The up and down motion of their tail flukes propels them through the water and allows them to jump in the air. Playful dolphins enjoy riding the bow of fast moving vessels where they can be pushed by the wave, surfing effortlessly.

Most dolphins have a curved dorsal fin and ventral flippers that vary in size and shape from one species to the next. Their beaks are well defined and they generally have conical teeth arranged in both the upper and lower jaws.

Dolphins riding the bow of the expedition vessel. It takes a quick breath through its blow-hole as it surfaces

Today the dolphin family is comprised of 35 different species that inhabit nearly every sea. Some species are only found in certain areas while others have a worldwide range. For instance the five species of river dolphins (Platanistoidea) live in specific river systems of the world. The Indus (*Platanista minor*) and Baiji (*Lipotes vexillifer*) river dolphins of India and China respectively are both threatened heavily by development and fishing and there are only a few hundred individuals left in defined river habitats. Conversly, common dolphin (*Delphinus delphis*) and pantropical spotted dolphin (*Stenella attenuata*) are found in all oceans and are the most abundant of the dolphin species, with populations estimated at 1 million and 2 million respectively . The offshore spinner dolphin (*Stenella longisrostris*) is most definitely the most agile and exuberant of the cetaceans, leaping and spinning as high as 6 metres in the air. The populations of coastal bottlenose dolphin (*Tursiops truncatus*) have been exploited by man for oceanariums, navy missions and food.

The dolphin's streamlined form enables it to move efficiently through the water

DOLPHINS, PORPOISES and all toothed whales have an advanced sixth sense called echolocation which uses a system of sonar similar to bats. The dolphin emits a series of 'clicks' from the upper nasal passage located in the rounded forehead, known as the melon. Echolocation informs the dolphin of the size, shape and movement of an object. The clicks are reflected off any object and received back as echoes through the animal's lower jaw and into the inner ear. The method of echolocation in dolphins is similar to the sonar used on boats to detect schools of fish or the ultrasound scanners used in hospitals to check unborn babies.

The reason for the dolphin's constant gracious smile was discovered to be related to functions of echolocation. The lower jaw of the dolphin curves outwards to serve as a sound conducting ear. Using this feature, the 'clicks' emitted by the melon can be heard by other dolphins several miles away.

This extraordinary sensory mechanism of echolocation allows dolphins to find flatfish and crustaceans completely buried in the sand. They can also catch fast-swimming prey in total darkness. The short and repetitive clicks, estimated at less than 1 millisecond in duration, can temporarily stun a fish, allowing the dolphin to grasp it easily. It was actually fishermen who first described the fishing methods of dolphins. They saw them effortlessly picking previously stunned fluttering fish from the surface.

The larger odontocetes, like the sperm whales, use echolocation as their main method of communication, their clicks being longer and repeated less often than those of the dolphin. Echolocation in dolphins is not the principal means of communication as dolphins have their own language in the form of whistles. Studies of dolphin whistles within the same species revealed that different groups will have their own whistle dialect. Furthermore, each individual will have a signature whistle or voice print that dolphins probably use to recognize each other. Using a computer to digitalize recordings from an underwater video camera, Dr Denise Herzing has created an electronic dictionary of signature whistles of the Atlantic spotted dolphin (*Stenella frontalis*). Vocalization in dolphins is still, however, poorly understood and will require many more years of research.

Echolocation allows dolphins to find fish buried under the sand

Wild Dolphin Expeditions

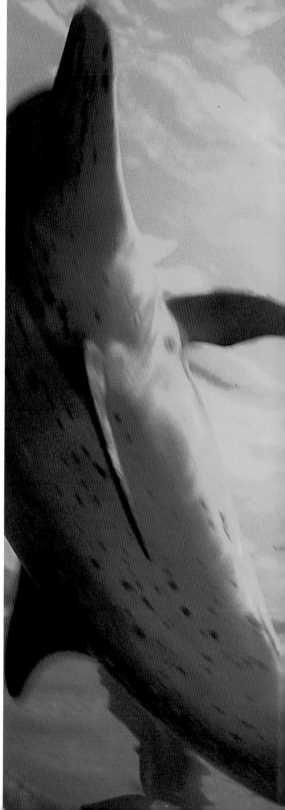

I SLAND EXPEDITION has been observing and documenting the population of wild Atlantic spotted dolphins found along the edge which separates the deep water of the Gulf Stream from the shallow Little Bahama Bank.

Primarily, the objectives of the dolphin expeditions have been to provide an opportunity for students to observe dolphins directly in the wild and to photograph and video their complex behaviour. Recently the expedition has been investigating the feasibility of establishing a sanctuary for the protection of the Atlantic spotted dolphins. Island Expedition has noticed a significant increase in boating activity in this area that may affect the dolphins in years to come.

The interaction between dolphin and man which occurs in The Bahamas is unique in the world and therefore it is essential to establish proper management of the area to ensure that the dolphins will not be disturbed because of man's indulgence.

This unmatched area where the resident spotted dolphins interact with people is 35 miles off the western shores of Grand Bahama. The crystal clear water on a sparkling white sand ridge allows for very spectacular photographs and film and some incredible encounters between dolphin and man. A small selection of extracts from articles written by students describe these experiences.

Man and dolphin interactions

Whenever you are looking for dolphins, wanting to be with them, anticipating their appearance – they are not there. Only when you have let go of all desires and expectations do they suddenly appear. Miraculously, we had found them, or they had found us. We hurriedly put on our gear and entered into their world. Here we are entering their world, and they not ours – they can swim off at their own will, but they stay to smile and play. They swirl, dart and swim around you, and at other times are docile and perform slow ballet-like movements up to the surface.

FROM 'THE SEA – THEIR WORLD, NOT OURS' BY RICHARD BEEK, SOUTH AFRICA

We cautiously entered the water and swam slowly towards them. They swam through my legs, over and under me. They were so beautiful. Nicolas advised us not to touch them or chase them, but at one point they came so close to me that I could not avoid touching them. They are so soft and smooth.

FROM 'AN ADVENTURE WITH WILD DOLPHINS' BY RAINO ENEAS, THE BAHAMAS

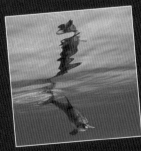

It seemed they loved to make us laugh and do silly things. Some of them turned on their backs and under the water their stomachs looked neon. They made beautiful tiny noises that we could hardly hear. They jumped around and fought with each other. In the last few minutes we had with them they jumped in groups of about four, circled us and dashed off.

FROM 'PLAYFUL DOLPHINS' BY AMBER CORVILLE, AGED 14, USA

Balletic movements

104

THE ATLANTIC SPOTTED DOLPHIN (*Stenella frontalis*) is one of five species of *Stenella* that live in temperate to tropical regions of the world. *Stenella* originates from the Greek word *stenos* meaning narrow, which is a common characteristic of the beaks of all *Stenella*. *Frontalis* refers to the prominent forehead of this dolphin. *S. frontalis* was first described by F. Cuvier off the west coast of Africa.

It is the common name 'spotted dolphin' that best describes this dolphin which as an adult is speckled with dots. The amount of dots determines the age of the spotted dolphin – the more dots the older the individual. It is the only cetacean that completely changes its colour pattern from newborn to adult. The tip of the rostrum (beak) becomes white with age, especially in the males.

Adult Atlantic spotted dolphins are approximately 2 metres in length and weigh up to 140 kilograms. In The Bahamas they have been observed feeding in the shallow sandy bottom on flounders, razorfish and tilefish, but will also venture in the deeper Gulf Stream to catch squid and pelagic fish. The dolphin reaches maturity between 12 and 15 years of age and has a one year gestation period. As with most cetaceans, babies are born tail first and will feed on their mother's milk. Other dolphins referred to as 'aunties', which may not be related to the calf, will also take the responsibility for teaching young dolphins how to survive.

Jo Jo the bottlenose dolphin

JO JO THE AMBASSADOR DOLPHIN of the Turks and Caicos islands is a rogue bottlenose dolphin that enjoys the company of humans. Island Expedition students have been fortunate to swim with Jo Jo. Dean Bernal, the executive director of the Dolphin, Whale and Wildlife project has maintained very close contact with Jo Jo. He monitors his health and makes sure tourists and locals are aware of the guidelines to follow when interacting with Jo Jo. As shown on the photo below Jo Jo is heavily scarred from encounters with motor boat propellors.

Mother and calf spend many years together. The Atlantic spotted dolphin acquires its spots gradually as it matures

Jo, Jo, ambassador dolphin of the Caribbean

Dolphin Etiquette

THERE IS NO SURE METHOD of attracting wild dolphins but it is best to wait and let the dolphins come to you. It appears that they are sometimes attracted to noises from engines, anchor chains or a diver on an underwater scooter. However if you are shooting underwater video, noises from boat engines or scooters affect the recording of the dolphin's whistle. Also the noise from the clicking and winding of students' disposable underwater cameras seemed to stir the dolphins' curiosity.

Once the dolphins choose to interact with you it is good to keep eye contact with them and try to follow them with gentle dolphin-like movements. Island Expedition and a number of other experts do not recommend reaching out with hands or touching dolphins as they may see this as a threat. There have however been several encounters where students could not resist stroking the belly of very calm dolphins who appeared to be enjoying it. As a rule it is best to refrain from such activities as no one has yet determined when the dolphins will react positively or negatively. There have been recorded incidents where dolphins have injured humans who handled them aggressively.

Over the years Island Expedition has found that it is best not to swim or stay with dolphins that are not interested. If dolphins are sighted and then approached it does not necessarily mean they are keen on playing with humans. Staying for extended periods of time (over 1 hour) with dolphins is also not recommended as their own natural behaviour, like feeding, mating and socializing, should not be interfered with. Dolphins are very complex social animals that should be respected at all times.

Interaction with humans

Captive Dolphins

CONSIDERING THE NUMBER of international organizations and people that are opposed to dolphins in captivity, it is surprising that there are still numerous captive dolphin facilities worldwide.

It is important to note that when dolphins are captured for amusement parks, swim with dolphin programmes, and the navy, this may not only kill or injure dolphins, but also disturb the entire pod. Dolphins are highly social animals that live and interact together in groups. They feed and play together. They communicate and interact with each other, they form very tight packs to protect themselves from predators such as sharks and orcas, they protect pregnant females, assist with birth and nurture their young for years.

The dolphin's traumatizing experience of being captured and separated from its family, placed in a small pen, fed dead fish by hand and forced to follow the rules of its captors, affects its natural instincts. Rehabilitation is therefore very complicated, costly and requires re-teaching the dolphin all it used to know in its natural world. For example, the dolphin must be taught that fish is essential food for survival and not a reward for performing for its captors.

The simple fact that a number of dolphin experts and ex-dolphin trainers have become anti-captive dolphin activists, should be enough to prove to the world that we no longer need to keep them caged.

Gail Woon is a Bahamian marine biologist with 14 years' experience in the United States, Australia and The Bahamas who joined Island Expedition on several journeys to observe wild whales and dolphins. She worked in the marine mammal industry at a 'Dolphin Experience' for 18 months. The following are quotes from an article, 'Dolphins are not disposable items', Gail Woon published in the local paper in response to a pro-captive dolphin letter.

We used to tell the guests that the pink areas of the base of the pectoral fins on two of the animals were their armpits. Later on it was revealed to me that those were scars from their capture. The capture process is not pretty. Some animals are drowned or their fins broken and because they are damaged they are discarded; their chances of survival are next to nil.

If you think about taking an intelligent animal and putting it in a small pen, taking it away from its family, and its freedom to roam far and wide into different depths of ocean, can you call this ecotourism? I think not!

Interaction between dolphins

Dolphins in Danger

THE WORLD'S DOLPHIN POPULATION is declining rapidly and man is entirely responsible for this. Man has generated marine debris of which plastics and discarded fishing gear have the worst effect on dolphins. Plastics float around the globe for an eternity. Dolphins die from eating plastics and get tangled up in discarded fishing line, ropes and nets. Marine debris, however, does not claim nearly as many dolphins as pollutive toxins and certain fishing methods.

The ancient coastal method of fishing using gill nets stretched out for miles on buoys has claimed countless dolphins. Fish enter the net head first and are trapped by their own gills when trying to withdraw. Dolphins do the same and are caught by their teeth and fins and drown. For the most part, the dolphins are not even desired by the fishermen and are considered 'bycatch'. It has been estimated that 1 million or more dolphins and porpoises die each year in these types of net.

Some of the modern methods of fishing, especially in the tuna industry, have taken a great toll on dolphins. The use of up to 40-mile-long monofilament drift nets to encircle and trap tuna was fortunately banned in 1992. This move was partly initiated by a secret video tape made by Samuel LaBuddle on board a tuna fishing boat which showed the horrific number of dolphins slaughtered using this method. This led to the drive for companies to sell only 'dolphin safe' canned tuna.

Pollution from toxins is probably of the greatest concern for both dolphins and man. Scientists are finding that increasing numbers of dolphins die from biological infections (viruses or bacteria) possibly triggered by high levels of chemical toxins such as polychlorinated biphenyls (PCBs). PCBs are dangerous non-biodegradable chemicals found in paint thinner, batteries and electrical transformers and they have made their way to the sea. It is believed that the PCBs, injested through the consumption of contaminated fish, are lowering the immune system of dolphins and other marine mammals leading to diseases such as skin lesions, brain tumours and cutaneous herpes. Even though PCBs and other hazardous chemicals have been banned from major polluting countries, these are still present in land dumps and can leach into the sea through the rivers.

Many will argue that there are enough problems on earth without having to worry about the health of dolphins but because dolphins are higher up on the marine food chain, they are accumulating a greater amount of toxins. If dolphins are contracting more and more diseases and are being affected by more and more pollutants then this is an indication of the state of the sea and the future of an important resource to man. Kenneth S. Norris, a dolphin expert who has devoted his life to observing and researching dolphins since the early 1950s, says it all in a few words 'The dolphin's fate has become a gauge of where the entire earth stands.'

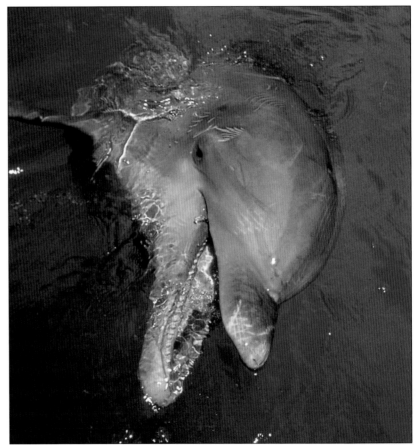

The fixed grin of a dolphin is very deceptive. This highly social and intelligent animal suffers greatly in captivity

Dolphins petting

Y OU WILL NOT DISCOVER new oceans unless you have
the courage to lose sight of the shore.

Expedition vessel **Simpatico**

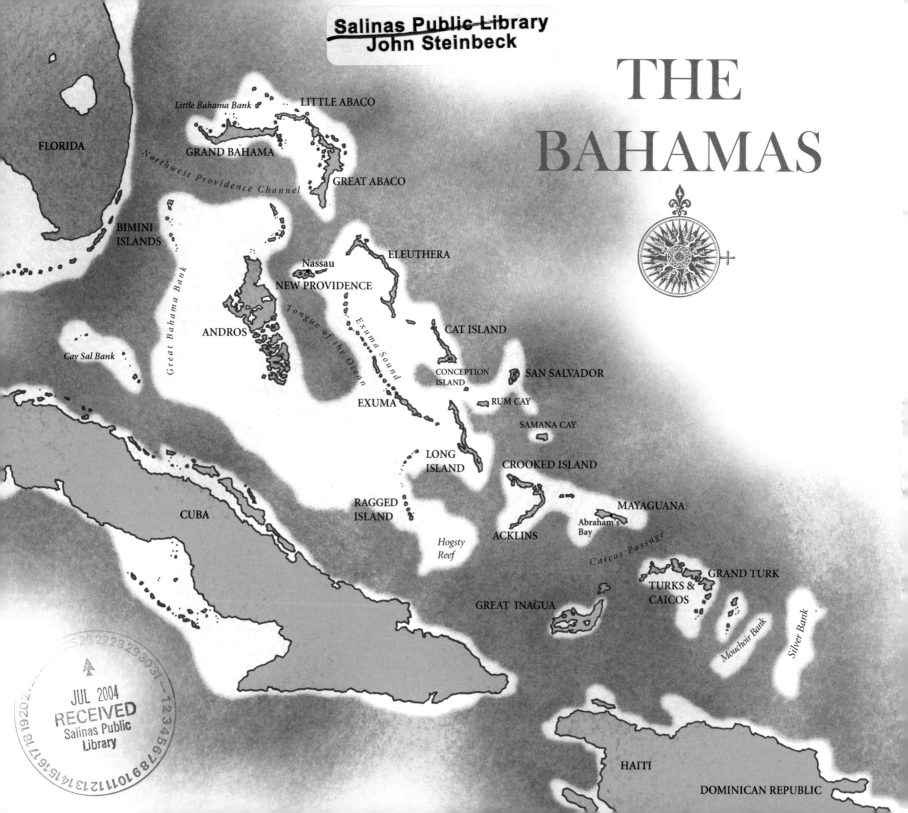

THE BAHAMAS

FLORIDA

Little Bahama Bank   LITTLE ABACO

GRAND BAHAMA

Northwest Providence Channel

GREAT ABACO

BIMINI
ISLANDS

ELEUTHERA

Great Bahama Bank

Nassau
NEW PROVIDENCE

Tongue of the Ocean

Exuma Sound

ANDROS

CAT ISLAND

Cay Sal Bank

CONCEPTION
ISLAND

SAN SALVADOR

RUM CAY

EXUMA

SAMANA CAY

LONG
ISLAND

CROOKED ISLAND

MAYAGUANA

RAGGED
ISLAND

Abraham's
Bay

ACKLINS

CUBA

*Hogsty
Reef*

Caicos Passage

GRAND TURK

TURKS &
CAICOS

GREAT INAGUA

Mouchoir Bank

Silver Bank

HAITI

DOMINICAN REPUBLIC